Without Woman or Body

poems by

Allison Field Bell

Finishing Line Press
Georgetown, Kentucky

Without Woman or Body

ACKNOWLEDGMENTS

Thanks to the following journals for publishing my work:

Ruminate: "Girl in My Youth"
Palette Poetry: "Sonoran Desert"
Superstition Review: "Ketura"
Sugar House Review: "Garden"
Aquifer: The Florida Review Online: "Weight of Water"
The Greensboro Review: "Anatomy Lesson"
RHINO Poetry: "coalesce"
Shō Poetry Journal: "Barcelona, 2008"
Passages North: "Teacup Rose" and "Horse Girl"
THRUSH Poetry Journal: "Four Walls Become a Woman"
Lunch Ticket: "You have to run open mouthed"
The Paddock Review: "How to Write a Poem Without *Woman* or *Body*"

Publisher: Leah Huete de Maines
Editor: Christen Kincaid
Cover Art: Allison Field Bell
Author Photo: Sam Thilen
Cover Design: Elizabeth Maines McCleavy

Order online: www.finishinglinepress.com
        also available on amazon.com

Author inquiries and mail orders:
Finishing Line Press
PO Box 1626
Georgetown, Kentucky 40324
USA

Contents

Garden

I haven't been honest with myself. The peony in my front
yard had just one bloom last year. Fleeting, fuchsia.

I watched it unfurl one petal at a time, breaking through the bud.
Couldn't leave the house for fear of it happening without me.

Stared through the window in my pajamas. Days lost to waiting.
My doctor wants to increase my medication—he suggests we double it,

my brain needs more than it already has. I think about the quartet of tulips
in the backyard—every winter I fear they must have died down there

but every spring they shoot through the ground in a great miracle—
green stalks and deep wine-red blossoms. I tell my doctor this. A metaphor.

When really, I wonder how long any of us can last. Winters changing: rain in
February in Utah. The whole of the Salt Lake Valley under threat.

Beneath the lake's liquid skin: poison. The last medication I tried flooded
my heart in a ruthless double-beat. I couldn't do anything right:

drink coffee, pour wine. I yelled at my doctor on the phone. He agreed
that it was wrong. Told me I shouldn't be drinking. Too much

for my liver to hold. There's also a bed of irises that bloom
later than the rest: early summer and their pale pink flesh opens

to the mountain heat. Doctor doesn't understand why I'm talking
about bulbs, about flowers. Why I can't just say I want to get better.

I tell him, I wish I could just live outside. Plant me in the yard, let me
disappear in winter and return come spring. Let me be brief and full of light.

Horse Girl

As a child, I raised guppies. Bright scaled creatures that fluttered through freshwater. They multiplied overnight, filling the tank with color. I netted the babies to separate them, so they wouldn't be consumed. When they were big enough, I sold them for a few dollars to a local pet store. I was saving to buy a horse. A useless enterprise. I wanted something to carry me across the earth. All that muscle. Large liquid eyes. The smell of alfalfa and hay. Instead, I had cages. Tanks. Green anoles, hermit crabs, a teddy bear hamster, the guppies. My room a menagerie of what I could afford. The horse I dreamed up was a proud unbroken mare. And I wouldn't be the one to break her—no one would—but she would only respond to me. My touch. My voice. A way of being something other than myself. Maybe every little girl's fantasy. I didn't know how to be in the world otherwise. Makeup, shaved legs, boys. But I wasn't a horse girl either. I was guppy girl. I saved the boldest most beautiful males for breeding. Their tails a spectacle. Watching them shimmer. Running the numbers in my head. Heart in a gallop.

Beneath the Roots

My mother says I've seen the world,
She says, *Look at all the places you've been.*

She says, *And all the homes you've made.*
In Salt Lake City, I'm digging a hole in my backyard.

I don't know what it's for but I know it will be
bigger. As a child, I believed I could dig

myself to another country, another world.
Little girl fingers clawing through earth.

Every evening, my mother scrubbed my nails
clean. Laughing one day, cursing another.

Her moods as mercurial as the weather. Full of heat
and then rain and then cold California night.

This hole in my backyard started out about grass. Dig down
beneath the roots. Grass in a high desert. Grass in a drought.

The hole is to my waist. Jump in every morning and remove
shovelfuls before work. Cool damp dirt at my sides. Imagine

being buried in it. Worms curling through my toes,
the unbearable pressure. My mother says it's wonderful

that I've traveled, that I am so adventurous. To live
in Indiana / New Mexico / Arizona / Utah. To live

in Ecuador / Israel / Greece / England. To follow my impulse.
She doesn't know how difficult it is to leave the house.

Check the stove, the door, the cat. Recheck and recheck
and recheck. I cannot see beyond the digging. The hole

looks like a trap like a home like a portal. Soon, I will
not be able to crawl my way out. Suspended below

the edges of the surface. Fantasize an airplane,
a train, a car. Something with motion and the in-between,

not quite home but not quite somewhere else. Here, I will
let go. Cat meowing, doors wide open, stove burners alight.

What it means to leave a place and to arrive. Hide out
until the sun rises in another time zone. Until I feel the damp

dew of morning. Don't know where I am anymore,
bare feet chilled and covered in the dirt that made me.

You have to run open mouthed
after "Frida Kahlo to Marty McConnell"

to winter. Your body is Indiana
strung between better states.
You found a man who thought
everything worthy was broken,
wanted to fix roofs and engines
and you, foolish girl. Now you must
dismantle his story. Run to the
desert and bury your heels in
the waterless earth. Let your nights
be long and whiskey-weathered. Let
men touch you who don't deserve
hands and then tell them that.
Crush chilies in your kitchen,
cook them into sauce into
your lips. Wear lace on the outside.
Let your hair grow long. Tattoo
your neck, your chest, your thighs.
Stupid girls are always trying
to scrub their skin clear.

And you are not stupid. You are full
of knots, ringed with memory.
You have legs as resilient as cacti
and you can plant them anywhere.

Ketura

I.
Dusk
  copper cloaked, acacia
    silhouettes. I'm
  in my freebox skirt,
             cut-sleeve t-shirt. Glass
of arak,   mint leaf suspended
  above ice.   here, now,
the worst worry   is animal.
  Snake,   spider,   solifuge.
    I   wander among rocks,
        sipping, watching my
  skin go gold.

II.
Just last night,
      I had   a man here, out
  in the   desert,   at the date palm
    roofed   mud hut, built
      by children. He dragged
a mattress   out to
    fuck me.   Now, in the dust,
  alone,   I practice saying
no.   *No thank you,*   I say
  to the warm evening air.
    I kick a rock, watch it
stir   up a tiny cloud.

III.
  Wasn't   even him
    I wanted.   His girlfriend:
long   black hair, laughter
      contagious. I didn't know
   how to say that either.   How
   to think it.   She will not
forgive me.   She will call
me *American slut.*   *American*
    whore. Bitch.   Later
still,   she will marry him,
   have his two children.

IV.
Right now,   alone,   I
                can hear   the military in
             their adjacent desert.   Distant
          crack of weapons.   This place:
          riddled with war.
            Stars flicker
to life.   Soon the sky   will be full
  of them.   Soon, I will be
            back   on the kibbutz,
confessing.   I will drink
               arak with men,   smoke
               nargila with men. I
       will feel the night
               change, air cooler,
          stars brighter.

Barcelona, 2008

Your hair is bright blonde to your
ass. Six months of desert sun. Six months of
nargila arak Hebrew Arabic. Here, you can
speak. You can read signs, order a glass of wine.
Vino, por favor. You can ask for directions, tell
men to fuck off. You're fatter than you want to be,
but aren't you always? Tonight, a woman wants
you. Dark haired, white polka dots on a black dress.
Takes your hand. Skin so soft you think you might
fall through it. Leads you through a crowd
of men to the street. Lights two cigarettes.
Your hair is sun, she says in English. You smile,
inhale. It's not the truth: this calm, cool
inhale. Your own hand wet and trembling.
You're too young and dumb and afraid
to look at her the way she looks at you.
Her name is Eva. She kisses your cheek,
you blush. You leave her in the street, feel her
eyes on your back. You don't turn around.

To Think That I Could Be a Mother

Streets with their dramatic peaks and valleys, fog that buries skyscrapers and the great gold bridge over choppy gray water. This is the city at night, and you're drunk. You've started at a bar and then a friend's house. You're in the street now, at an intersection with a bottle. You take the last swig and throw the bottle up in the air, its clear glass refracts the streetlights—a floating crystal, it kisses the telephone wires and shatters back down. Your friends are not impressed. They shake their heads at your destruction. You want to explain how the bottle left your hands, how sometimes bottles do. You want them to understand tonight when you try to steal the champagne from the Safeway on Market, you are and are not trying to prove something. You want them to understand when you run through the train tunnel, you do and do not have something to lose. And when you sleep in Dolores Park, your friend's jacket a shared blanket, three chihuahuas nipping you awake to a clear hungover morning, you want them to know you're not sure where the line is and when and how far you've crossed over it.

Sonoran Desert

At night, a dreamscape of   shapes,

      spikes   gone soft   in starlight.

trail   between their   water-logged

      forms   luminous. Proud saguaro   sentinels:

      stand up straight,   stand up straight.

I haven't   come to the desert   for its beauty,

      but for   its scarcity. The way water   pools

      and streams   out across   great swaths of land.

I want to know   what it's like to live   without

      something.   Not something,   but someone.

      Stars   spilled like salt   across the table of sky.

The fresh clean   creosote   smell. Soft glowing

      teddy bear cholla,   wraith-like   ocotillo limbs,

      indistinct   clumps of brittle bush.   Coyotes in the

distance.   Moonrise over mountains,   sucking up

      stars,   turning the world   silver.   I think about

      how just yesterday   I wanted   to sleep

forever.   This is what my therapist calls   death.

      But I wonder.   We say forever   when we mean

      for as long   as we can   stand. Sometimes,

that isn't long   at all. Bats   slip like shadows through the air.   I should turn around now,

but before me   is a forest   of silhouettes,

a study   in mortality,   a great open desert   full

and awake   and belonging   to no one.

Teacup Rose

Yesterday by the teacup roses, I lost sight of myself. I stared down at my arms—streaked with blood from deadheading the front yard. I didn't recognize my limbs. Not my legs, not my elbows or biceps or wrist bones. It seemed so easy, for a moment, to be something else. A man perhaps. In leather gloves and spandex, out in front of my house on a Monday. The petals of the large pink rose fell to the ground, a littering of beauty. Their satin skin strewn across the succulents. My partner thinks to rake them up, to dispose of them, but I refuse. Too much like romance: a scatter of petals on a bed. My partner doesn't like roses. Too much the flower of boomers, he says. He likes the teacup rose best though, if he had to choose. So unlike the rest. Small buds, scentless, low to the ground. There by the roses he doesn't hate, I wondered if he would prefer me someone else. A dancer. A journalist. A woman with a career and an exercise routine. I studied my legs: the thighs, the kneecaps, the shin bones. I slipped into that other reality: man. Then I stared at the flawless tiny red blossoms, unlocked the shears and began.

How to Write a Poem Without *Woman* or *Body*

Use the words *girl* or *female*. Write about fingertips
and elbows. But don't forget this cage of muscle and
bone, the familiar and unfamiliar feel of eyes on legs,
eyes on breasts, eyes on ass. The ways in which you
can never relinquish your sex. If you were a man
you would smile with your head down to the pavement.
Catch every door for every person wanting to pass through.
Remember that your body (there it is) moves over
sidewalks with ease. But you are not a man, you are
a woman (and there she is). You did not design yourself
this way. Breasts and hips. You wish it were otherwise.
That your body (and again) was a flat straight line.
A neutral grace to your step. (A fantasy.) You don't mean
to write poems about bodies (or women), you just
mean to write poems. You can write about trees—
the cypress on the cliffs (Was it Santa Cruz?), their jagged
wind-bent branches. Cottonwoods (in so many arroyos)
in New Mexico or the ones that lean over that park path
in Salt Lake. Or maybe return to the Sonoran Desert
(that you love so dearly). Cholla piling up to the sun,
prickly pear scattered across dirt. Stop collapsing in
(on yourself), finding ways to make metaphors about
kneecaps, about skin. What is it like to watch the world (melt)?
the body (of a woman) walking. Kicking through piles
of yellow gingko leaves in Indiana. Waiting for winter. (Waiting.)

The Farm

Carob tree in the center, its curling pods. And strange lines like roots dangling from branches. Color in distinct swaths, earth tones. Tones of the land. Two buildings on either side, one an animal enclosure, the other a barn. And between them a path leading to a woman. I wonder about that woman. I wonder about myself, standing before the painting. In London, though I remember it being Paris. Hemingway's favorite painting. I read a story about him buying it, and imagine it strapped to the roof of a car. He kept it above his bed. I know the image I kept above mine. A photograph: an eagle hunter in Mongolia. The same clear blue sky. A block of blue. Negative space. In the painting, a moon. In the photograph, nothing. Just sky and the half-silhouette of a man with an eagle. Wings outstretched. A man painted the painting, a man took the photograph too. An Israeli man who touched me in my sleep, uninvited. And then I frame and hang his photograph above my bed. Just like I'm not supposed to love Hemingway. A man's man. The books too direct, too violent, too much for my womanness. And yet, I like the painting because of him. Hemingway's favorite. I like the photograph because of him: a warning. Memory of a man in the sheets. Memory of his touch. Memory of waking. Memory of what the fuck. Memory of standing in front of the painting. I don't notice the lizard in the foreground, the agave along the path. Hands where I don't want them. Memory of anger. Memory at a museum looking.

coalesce

And the dew on the grass after a night full up of air from the Pacific,
    it's there glittering like translucent pearls, like tiny bodies clinging.

And the feeling of teeth against knuckle, two fingers
    probing the back of your throat: you should stop, you should stop.

And the redwood trees outside the house,
    the stick-straight tall of them. Soft bark, feathered leaves.

And you in the bathroom, staring down the mirror, pull at the flesh
    of the hips, suck in the stomach, raise the jaw away from the neck.

And outside is spring again. Daffodils freed from their winter slumber,
    apple trees and plum trees and apricot alive with blossom.

And you are afraid he might hear you so you run the sink,
    the shower as though California had water enough forever.

And in the backyard, spilling over the fence line in the summertime,
    are the blackberries, the berries you love best, plump and dense and sweet.

And the fruit taking over blossom like a woman undressing
    in moonlight. Moon in the window and the room and you with your body

and afraid of what it could hold if you let it.

Looking at Your Body

One
Ache. A hollowing out. Remember the time with the woman who ordered marrow from the menu. Two bones balanced on a plate. How you spooned and sucked at the insides. Fat and blood. The bone at your lips.

Two
Unworry your fingers from their knot. Skin and knuckle. Clamped together. Pressure. You could be so much more if you wanted.

Three
Fever dream. A man on a rooftop hurling himself through the air to another rooftop. Your indecision at the edge. All that space. The pavement below. The woman who pulled you back, saying, *Don't be stupid. Don't.* Day you realized something about women: trust.

Four
Deceit and desire and desire and desire. The lover in your trembling arms, in the frozen Midwest winter. And the trees outside skeletons. And inside the room is ice and the way the two of you fit and do not fit together.

Five
Undo the expectations of your appendages. Feet attached by a kind of hinge. Tendon and bones settled into each other. Toe pointed, ankle flexed. Line from shin to toe: an exclamation mark.

Six
Remember the tragic falling of that bird's nest. Sparrows or finches. Something small and unmemorable. Still, you saw the dog and screamed. It swallowed the barely-feathered babies whole, smacking its lips.

Seven
Breathe. Difficult at altitude. That thinness, the tilted mountains—jagged, snow-capped. Slick wet rocks, landscape studded with wildflowers. You couldn't find your way home if you tried.

Eight
Sleep with the stranger at the bar, the stranger at the restaurant, the stranger with the wife, with the husband. You're not that kind of woman.

Nine

Sometimes it's better to pretend: your niece and your nephew with the pillow fort. One of them insists, *This is mine.* The other insists, *This is mine.*

Ten

Behind the wheel, ninety on the 101. Ocean crashing to one side. You could be anywhere, but you're here. In California with your history and your lover and a car full of you and your will to escape.

How is this Supposed to End

Beneath the table, arms crossed
over my belly: this food isn't for me.

No food is.
I am not eating. Not salmon or rice or broccoli.
I drink wine. Deep red stains
on my teeth, my lips.

They do not talk to me: my mother,
her best friend and the husband.

Then, suddenly, they do. Or: he does.
The husband. The man.
He's drunk on beer and sunlight. His face
irredeemably red.

                    What if you slept in my bed?

We women study our plates, mine full, theirs empty.
I hold my belly tighter: a torniquet.

He is like an uncle to me. As a child,
I sat in his lap. His wife changes the subject:

                    Are you going to eat that?

I shake my head.
But he, the husband, the man, my uncle,
persists. To my mother, he winks,

                    Tonight, we can trade places

Earlier, he was speaking of my beauty. My hair,
my little female figure.

Before that, he was my uncle, folding me into
an embrace. Telling me how grown up I have become.
Now, he is drunk and I want: to be anything other than
woman.

It is smallness I desire. To become less
than I am. To turn sideways
and vanish. Press my belly to my spine.

I look at my full plate and then up at my uncle: his red drunk
face,
eyes with a certain ugly shimmer.
How is this supposed to end?

My mother says nothing.
But later, she locks the door to our room
and when she thinks I am sleeping: she slips

out of bed and checks it. Twisting
the brushed nickel one way
and then the other,
a small metal sound in the night.

Girl In My Youth

Before her, I liked them. Their volume, their strength. Girl in my youth pulled at her own muscle there, telling me too much body for one body. And: running makes us ugly. Legs manly. Carved calves, thick thighs, soccer player shin guard tan, slope down to the ankles, muscles I could flex. Defined and sturdy. She stood in front of the mirror: pinching, angling, sighing. Before her, I didn't want my body smaller. Before her, I didn't know I wanted to be like her. Her body, her legs. Her way of looking, hungry for some other body. Before her, I didn't know I wanted her. And after her too. For years, I didn't know how to want a body like mine. A girl can see another girl in the mirror, can fail to see the woman at her side.

Anatomy Lesson
after Ada Limón

You chop an onion across
from me, its edge in the air.
The strained, the quiet
muffled snowfall outside. For hours,
nothing but white beyond the window.
Your thoughts on anatomy,
the ways a body can break.
My study: the five noble grapes.
Sweetness, acidity, tannin, alcohol, body.
As a child, I was excited about daffodils,
stems unfurling from the earth,
soft white heads opening.
Paperwhites with their duplicitous
pale clusters. Large cupped ice follies
with their yellow centers. I beheaded
them all, filled a tray of water,
presented it to my mother. She shrieked,
I wept. The odor of onion drifting.
You ignore me and chop another:
isn't that enough? The luminous remains.
Chardonnay, Riesling, Sauvignon Blanc.
Heart, lungs, stomach, liver.
Later, you will practice on my body:
here the kidneys, there an artery.
Outside, the snow is picking up.
By morning, the driveway will be
thick with it. Night: this cold white
reckoning. And who doesn't know
the myth? Narcissus in love with his reflection,
two onions, on a cutting board, shattered.

Liberty Park

Corridor of London planetrees,
thin silvery trunks against new
spring grass. Legs churning

in motion: shoes slap pavement, rollerblades
cut across concrete. *Excuse me,* a woman
says, pushing a baby in a stroller.

I haven't run for six years now,
and I will not have children
of my own. Foot shaved and

reshaped, screwed back together wrong.
Arthritic joint, a persistent ache, failure to fix
what was broken. I do not want

children. Or rather, he does not, and I
am thirty-five and broke and bipolar
and in a park alone on a Saturday.

Also a Saturday when he underwent his
vasectomy. When I picked him
up from the clinic, and he confessed

no pain. Saturday, a week later, when he
was allowed to run again. At the same
park, we tried and failed together. My foot throbbing

past an autumn purple, its leaves still green
for the season. Today, I slide over:
the woman and her baby pass. Creamy light

on the London planetrees—which I had always
taken to be plain sycamores. London planetrees:
a hybrid, half-sycamore, half-right. I shift

my weight from the bad foot,
the woman and her baby vanish
around a corner of green ash.

Weight of Water

Yesterday at the kitchen sink, my lover told me again
how I can't do it right—load the dishwasher, wash the cast iron.
No soap, no scrubbing. My hands submerged in water, scalding.

Today, I'd rather be a fish. Scales, gills, unblinking eyes. Curl
around the toxic tentacles of that blooming mass: the anemone.
Brilliant orange and white stripes against the rainbow of reef.

None of that anxiety that dwells in the stomach, hollows it out, drops
it to the knees. The way my lover yelled when I panicked—
shook and shimmied. Too much, too much.

Too much pressure from the water above,
but not feeling the ear-popping ascent from the depths of
the sandy floor. Water crushing bones. A whole sea of it.

I'd like to be a shark. A predator. Free in my own kingdom.
Beast so ancient, so full of its own history, so full of its
own instinct. So full. So unlike the way I am. Sitting on the edge

of the bed now, my lover beyond a slammed door. I wonder
what it is to escape something. Where it is I could go. Beyond
the twist of whitewater, the shallow sand shelf to the deep

underbelly of sea, cold dark infinite. Bliss, all that water, swimming.

Four Walls Become a Woman

> *Who shall measure the heat and violences of the poet's heart when*
> *caught and tangled in a woman's body?* —*Virginia Woolf*

I can measure it here, where the morning light spills
across the page, and my legs are thrown into shadow.
Or there, where outside the window redwood trees
tower over wall, over roof, softening the rising sun.

I found myself in a book again, not me but my body.
This heavy thing they call woman. Another man writing
my inner monologue. Another man thinking about pregnancy,
motherhood. But what of the myriad ways I desire?

The urgency to fill a page with words. Sex, too, but sometimes
I'd rather just be alone in a forest. I imagine a cabin.
Jumble of tree trunks needing to be turned to firewood. Shirtless
as any man, with my axe, cracking open the orange centers.

Men write me as if they understand walls. Four walls:
a room for this woman's body. If I'm being an optimist:
my cabin. But most likely a track home in suburbia.
Ripe and full with another child. Wife. Mother.

Or perhaps a mistress, a temptress: riddled with desire
for him. The manic pixie dream of his dream. I'd be thin
as a waif in a fairytale. I'd smoke cigarettes, drink vodka.
I'd sleep on silk sheets and steal thongs from department stores.

We'd stay in hotels, order bottles of champagne. I'd tell him
I've done this for him, for his desire. I'd lie. Things I've done
for men: lie. On my back. On my belly. I am between his walls,
his hotel's sheets, our bodies not our bodies, together.

Between my walls, in my room, there is no body. Woman or otherwise.
My walls are my own. My words are of water, my windows, light.

With Thanks

My deepest gratitude to the mentors and teachers who have inspired me and coached me and cared for me despite the huge pain in the ass of a student that I am: Gary Young, Uri Gordon, Melanie Bishop, Sheila Sanderson, K.L. Cook, Zoe Hammer, George Crane, Larry Felson, Allison Lynn. And of course, I have to thank all the incredible faculty at New Mexico State University for making me the writer that I am today, especially: Coach Rus Bradburd, Connie Voisine, the late Lee K. Abbott, Evan Lavender-Smith, Richard Greenfield, the late Mark Medoff, Carmen Giménez, and Lily Hoang. Finally, thanks to Lindsey Drager for always being in my corner no matter what and to Jackie Osherow for seeing something in these poems and for all the life lessons and wisdom.

A special thanks to Pam Houston for her generous mentorship and her gorgeous words and to Writing by Writers for the incredible opportunities I've had to build community and share and write.

Thanks to the Taft-Nicholson Center for being the perfect place for poetry. And thanks to all the folks who fund and organize the Steffenson Cannon Fellowship. I could not have written this book without the generous support I've received.

Thank you to the folks at Finishing Line who believed in this book; especially thanks to Leah Huete de Maines, Mimi David and Christen Kincaid.

To my writing community and loves here in Salt Lake City: you have read my pages over and over again and you don't hate me. Yet. This little book is especially possible because of Jasmine Khaliq, Jamie Smith, and Matty Layne Glasgow. And to those who have read and re-read my words in workshop and beyond, especially: Jessica Tanck, Vitasta Singh, Meagan Arthur, Audrey Bauman, Jake Yordy, Chengru He, Aristotle Johns, and Garrett Biggs.

And to my greater writing community: Zeeda Anderson, who wrote poetry with me as a teenager; Evan Belknap, my original writing buddy; my NMSU crew—Brady Richards, Patrick Stockwell, Emily Alex, Josh Randall, Emily Cook, Brooke Sahni, Barry Pearce, and Marzie Ghasempour; my Writing by Writers loves—Chaya Ungar; Caro Kay, Shirley Chan, and Mark Gross. You all have been so invaluable to my writing and my life. Thank you.

To my two sisters in words and in life: Tara Westmor and Diana Clarke. Tara, who has always believed in my poetry more than I have and has dug herself deep into my family and my life. And Clarke, my instant soulmate, my most dedicated mentor, and my closest—though farthest away—friend. Tara and Clarke: none of these words would exist without you. I cannot thank you enough.

To Ilan Cohen and Tori and Sam and Luca: thank you for being part of my chosen family.

To my bestie, Lauren Wallace, and to Morgan, Theo, and Lee: you have been my SLC family and I love you so much. I would not still be standing if it weren't for you all. Thank you.

To Garrett Randall, for being my partner in play, for making me laugh like a little kid again, and for encouraging and believing in my writing. I'm so glad we found each other.

To my family, of course: you all have made me the human I am today. My incredible parents who have supported me despite myself and are my first and most loyal readers. To my brother, Joe, and my sister-in-law Char: thank you for always being there, for loving me, for giving me the cutest nephew on the planet. To my Aunt Pam and my Uncle Bill: my second parents, my life sages, and the best people to take a road trip with. To my cousin, Avrey, and to Meghan: thank you for opening your lives to me, for always answering when I need you, and for taking me in even at my worst. To Reese and Hana for our long chats and for always welcoming me into your home. And to Susan and MeeMaw and Jack and Johnny. To the Boyds and to Ted and Martina and Henry. Y'all make my family complete.

And finally to the next generation of my family: you won't read this until you're in your twenties at least (I hope), but know that I love you and you inspire me every day to be a better human: Carlin, Evrett, Harlan, Judah, and Eli.

Allison Field Bell grew up in northern California, but has spent much of her adult life in and around the Southwest. Her debut full-length collection, *All That Blue*, is forthcoming in 2026 also from Finishing Line Press. Her nonfiction chapbook, *Edge of the Sea*, was published by CutBank Books in 2025. Her prose appears or is forthcoming in *Best Small Fictions, Best Microfiction, SmokeLong Quarterly, DIAGRAM, The Gettysburg Review, River Teeth, The Adroit Journal, New Orleans Review, West Branch, Alaska Quarterly Review,* and elsewhere. Her poems appear in *The Cincinnati Review, Smartish Pace, The Pinch, Passages North, Palette Poetry, RHINO Poetry, The Greensboro Review, THRUSH Poetry Journal,* amongst others. Her visual works appear in *The Madison Review, Fugue, Alligator Juniper* and other journals and exhibitions. Find her and more of her work at allisonfieldbell.com.